D1442031

LIGHTNING BOLT BOOKS™

From Chalkboards to Computers
How Schools Have Changed

Jennifer Boothroyd

Lerner Publications Company
Minneapolis

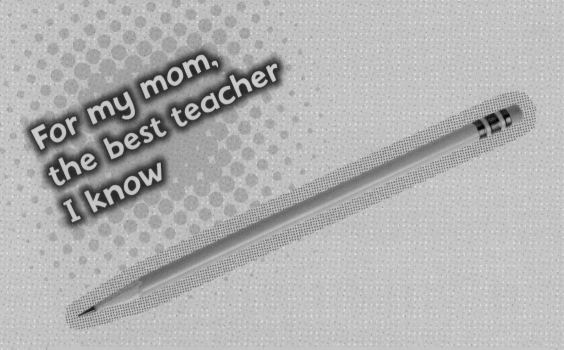

For my mom,
the best teacher
I know

Lerner Publications Company
A division of Lerner Publishing Group, Inc.
241 First Avenue North
Minneapolis, MN 55401 U.S.A.

Website address: www.lernerbooks.com

Library of Congress Cataloging-in-Publication Data

Boothroyd, Jennifer, 1972–
    From chalkboards to computers : how schools have changed / by Jennifer Boothroyd.
        p.   cm. — (Lightning bolt books™—Comparing past and present)
    Includes index.
    ISBN 978-0-7613-6744-4 (lib. bdg. : alk. paper)
    1. Schools—Juvenile literature. 2. Educational change—Juvenile literature. I. Title.
    LB1556.B65 2012
    371—dc22   2010048832

Manufactured in the United States of America
1 – CG – 7/15/11

Contents

What is School?

Children go to school to learn. They learn to read and write. They learn about math and science.

The ways children learn
have changed over time.
So have schools.

Around the School

In the past, a school had a library. Students came to borrow books.

Students used a tool called a card catalog to find books.

These days, schools have media centers. Students still borrow books. But they use computers too.

Computers help us learn new things.

In the past, students ate lunch in a cafeteria. Some students brought their lunches to school. Some students brought money to buy lunch.

These days, some people call cafeterias lunchrooms. Many students bring their lunches from home. Some use lunch accounts to buy food.

Kids store lunch money electronically in lunch accounts.

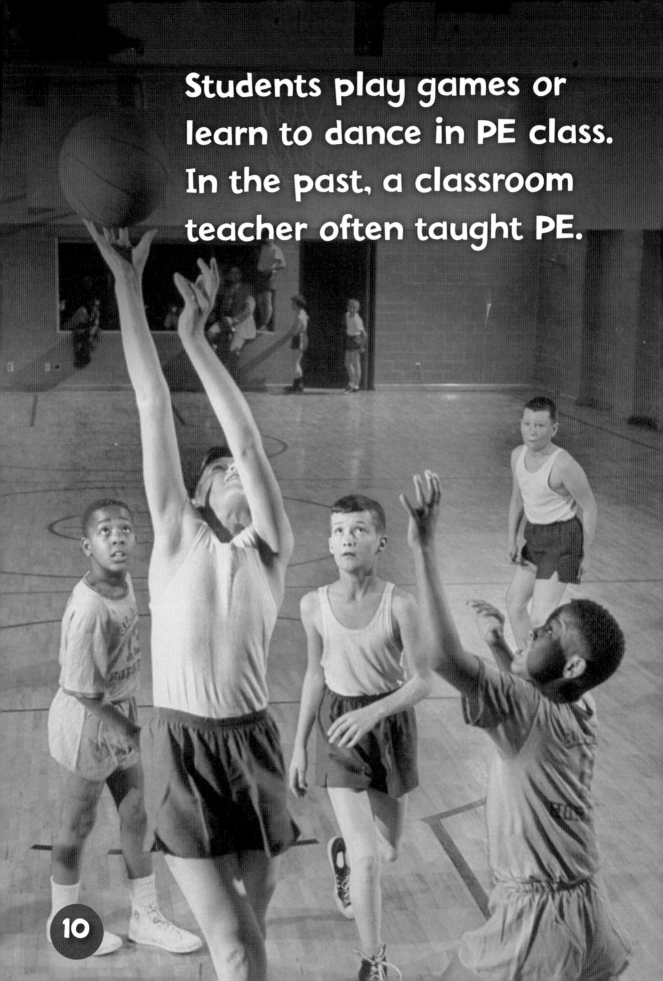

Students play games or learn to dance in PE class. In the past, a classroom teacher often taught PE.

These days, most schools have one or more PE teachers.

PE stands for "physical education."

School Tools

In the past, students carried books to school with a book strap.

These days, students use a backpack.

13

In the past, teachers wrote on chalkboards during lessons.

Things We Want to f
1. What the people eat.
2. Where they get their food.
3. What kinds of houses they build
4. The ways they travel.

If students caused trouble, teachers often asked them to clean the chalkboard erasers.

These days, teachers write on dry-erase boards. Some teachers use electronic boards too.

This board is connected to a computer.

In the past, teachers showed filmstrips about many topics.

Teachers played records or cassette tapes along with filmstrips.

These days, teachers
show films on DVD. Or
they use a computer and a
projector during lessons.

In the past, students carried their lunches in metal lunch boxes.

These days, students often use lunch bags made from foam and fabric.

Foam lunch bags keep food cold.

Ways to Learn

In the past, teachers taught students to add, subtract, multiply, and divide. These days, students still learn math skills.

In the past, students learned to read from a primer. This small book had drawings and short sentences.

A student practices reading in front of the class.

These days, students read
many kinds of books.
Sometimes the books have
photos instead of drawings.

In the past, students learned about places on Earth in geography class. They learned about events from the past in history class.

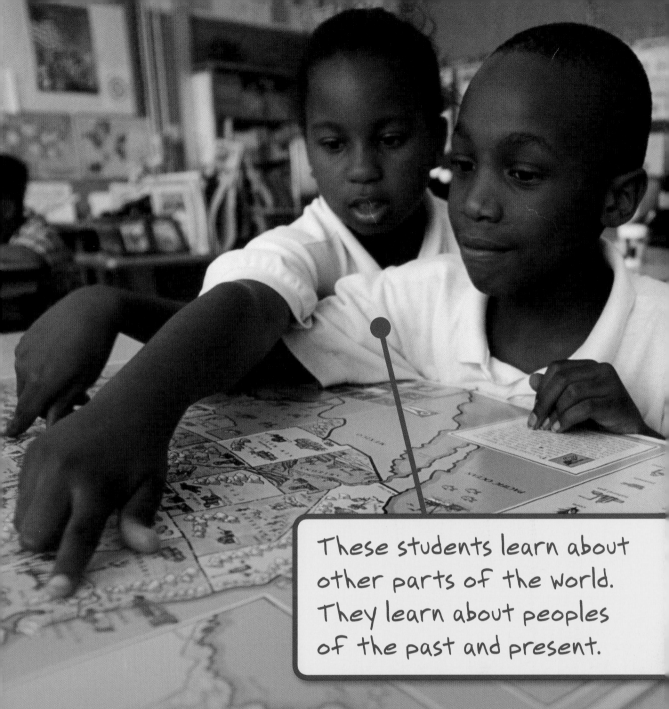

These students learn about other parts of the world. They learn about peoples of the past and present.

These days, teachers sometimes teach history and geography together. The class is called social studies.

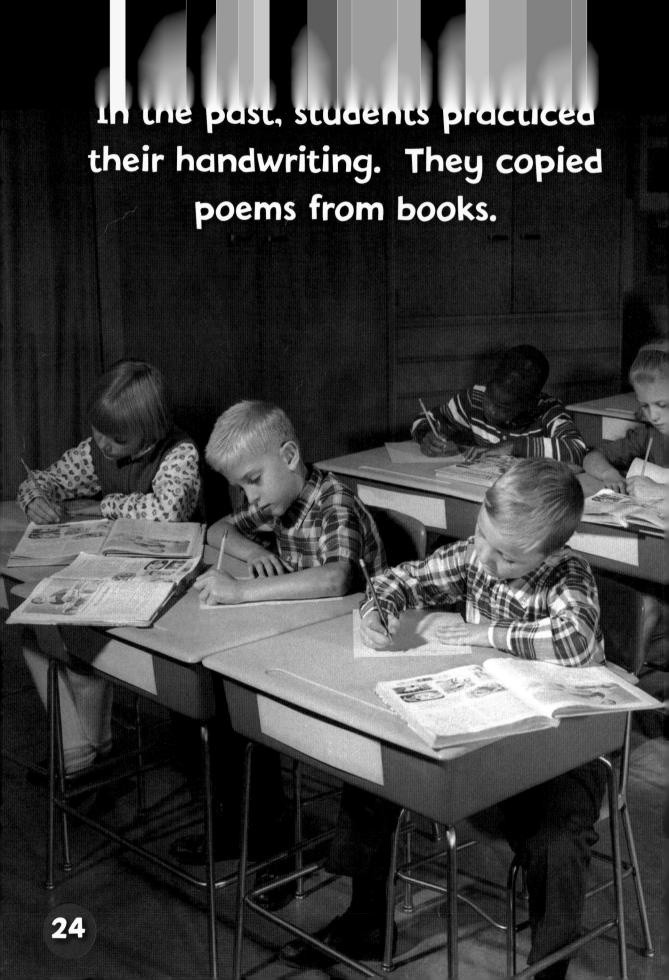

In the past, students practiced their handwriting. They copied poems from books.

These days, students still practice writing. But they spend time in keyboarding class too.

These students learn to type on a computer.

25

In the past, students learned about science. These days, they still do. They learn from textbooks. They try experiments.

During an experiment, a person does tests to learn information.

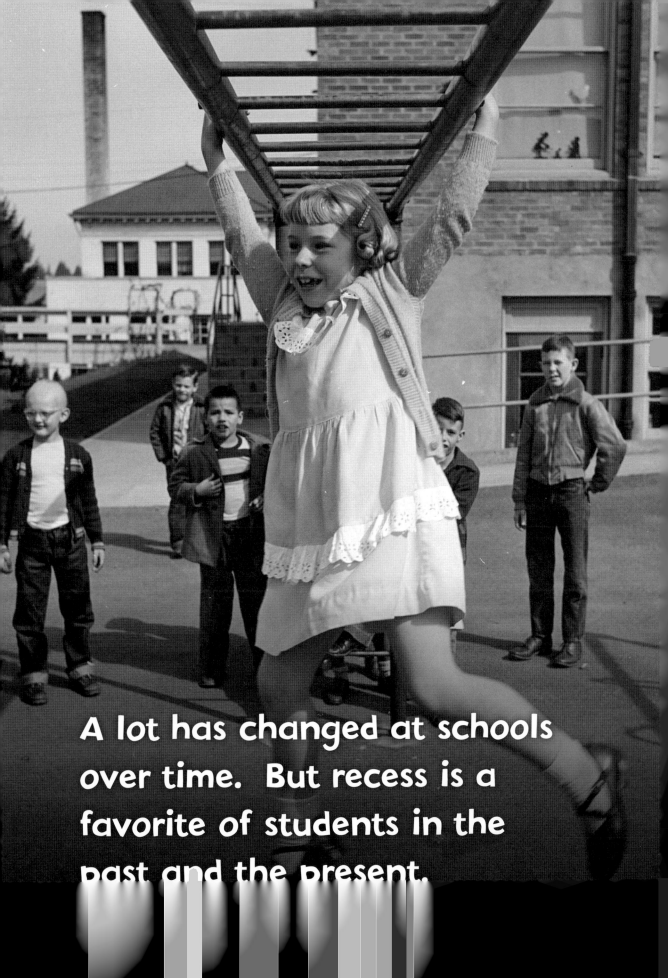

A lot has changed at schools over time. But recess is a favorite of students in the past and the present.

Names to Know

These people helped students grow.

Don Rawitsch, Paul Dillenberger, and Bill Heinemann: In 1971, these teachers invented the computer game *The Oregon Trail*. The game helps children learn history and math.

President Harry S. Truman: In the 1940s, many men were not healthy enough to serve in the U.S. Army. They had not eaten healthful food when

they were young. In 1946, President Truman began the National School Lunch Program. This program helped children eat healthful food at school.

Edwin Binney and **C. Harold Smith:**
In 1903, Edwin Binney and
C. Harold Smith invented a
wax crayon for children
to use. The first box
of Crayola crayons had
eight colors. They were black,
brown, blue, red, purple, orange,
yellow, and green.

Theodor Seuss Geisel: In the 1950s,
Theodor Geisel created a book for
children who were learning to read.
He wrote the book from
a list of 225 basic words.
The book was called
The Cat in the Hat. He
used the name Dr. Seuss.

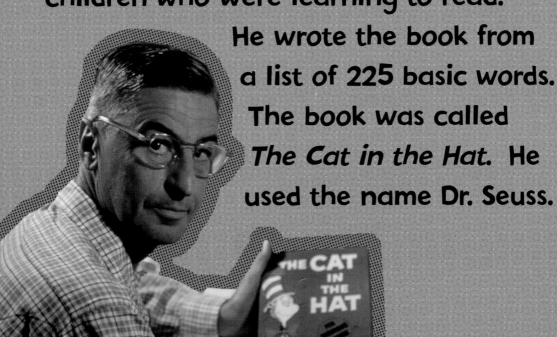

Glossary

cafeteria: a schoolroom where people prepare and eat food

experiment: a test to discover unknown information

filmstrip: a strip of film containing images that can be seen with a projector

geography: the study of Earth's countries, climates, and natural resources

keyboarding: learning to type on a computer keyboard

primer: a simple book used to teach reading

projector: a machine that shows images on a large surface

social studies: the study of history, geography, and government

textbook: a book used to teach a school subject

Further Reading

America's Story from America's Library
http://www.americaslibrary.gov/jb/index.php

Anderson, Sheila. *School.* Lerner Publications Company, 2008.

Heinz, Brian. *Nathan of Yesteryear and Michael of Today.* Minneapolis: Millbrook Press, 2007.

Rau, Dana Meachen. *Going to School in American History.* Milwaukee: Weekly Reader Early Learning Library, 2007.

Smithsonian National Museum of American History: Taking America to Lunch
http://americanhistory.si.edu/lunchboxes

Index

Photo Acknowledgments

The images in this book are used with the permission of: © Photodisc/Getty Images, p. 2; © Monkeybusiness/Dreamstime.com, p. 4; © Anderson Ross/Stockbyte/Getty Images, p. 5; © Don Cravens/Time & Life Images/Getty Images, p. 6; © Ariel Skeeley/Blend/Getty Images, p. 7; © Alfred Eisenstaedt/Time & Life Images/Getty Images, p. 8; © William Thomas Cain/Getty Images, p. 9; © Francis Miller/Time & Life Images/Getty Images, p. 10; © Big Cheese Photo LLC/Alamy, p. 11; © Phillip Gendreau/Bettman/CORBIS, p. 12; © Thomas M Perkins/Shutterstock Images, p. 13; © Harold M. Lambert/Archive Photos/Getty Images, p. 14; © David R. Frazier/Photolibrary, Inc./Alamy, p. 15; © Superstock/Getty Images, p. 16; © Altrendo Images/Stockbyte/Getty Images, p. 17; © George Marks/Stringer/Retrofile/Getty Images, p. 18 (top); © Leloft1911/Dreamstime.com, p. 18 (bottom); © dbtravel/dbimages/Alamy, p. 19; © Pat English/Time & Life Images/Getty Images, p. 20; © Gary John Newman/The Image Bank/Getty Images, p. 21; © Old Visuals/Alamy, p. 22; © Jorn Stjerneklar/Imagestate Media Partners Limited – Impact Photos/Alamy, p. 23; © H. Armstrong Roberts/CORBIS, p. 24; © Insy Shah/Gulfimages/Getty Images, p. 25; © Richard Lewisohn/Digital Vision/Getty Images, p. 26; © Vermilya/Stringer/Hulton Archive/Getty Images, p. 27; Library of Congress (LC–USZ62-98170), p. 28; © Jamie Pham Photography/Alamy, p. 29 (top); © Gene Lester/Archive Photos/Getty Images, p. 29 (bottom); © Dmitry Rukhlenko/Dreamstime.com, p. 30; © Henry Groskinsky/Time & Life Images/Getty Images, p. 31.

Front cover: Lucien Aigner/CORBIS (top); © LWA/Dann Tardif/Blend Images/ Getty Images (bottom).

Main body text set in Johann Light 30/36.